BREAKING THE BUBBLE LINE

AN INTRODUCTION TO FLY FISHING FOR WOMEN ON THE WATER

AMANDA MARIE

Copyright © 2024 by Amanda Marie

Ebook - ISBN #:979-8-9912171-0-1
Paperback - ISBN #: 979-8-9912171-1-8

All rights reserved. No part of this publication may be reproduced, distributed, or transmitted in any form or by any means, including photocopying, recording, or other electronic or mechanical methods, without the prior written permission of the author, except in the case of brief quotations embodied in critical reviews and certain other noncommercial uses permitted by copyright law.

BELONGING IN THE WILDERNESS

I'm not here to bullsh*t you about fly fishing. For someone who is just getting started or wants to get started in the sport, there can be a lot of barriers to entry. Basic vocabulary and knowledge shouldn't be one of those barriers. This book is by no means comprehensive. It is a basic guide to get you started on the water and in the community. In the end, we all come to the river for our own reasons. Speaking for myself, I am here for peace, connection, and adventure. I am here for me. I wrote this book for the women who see other women out on the water and are equally in awe, intimidated, and think that's-cool-but-that-could-never-be-me. It can be, and it should be. You have a place out here. If you're like me, sometimes you need a little push out the door. Consider these stories, knowledge, and lessons the push that gets you over the threshold. You have a place, a belonging, in the wild and beautiful spaces of the world. Don't be afraid to claim it.

ABOUT THE AUTHOR – AMANDA MARIE

I was born and raised on the central coast of California and now live in southcentral Alaska with my partner and our adventure pup. An avid writer since childhood, I became distracted from the publishing world by academia, various career paths, and outdoor adventures. At the end of the day, I am just a dog mom who loves to learn, read, and sit in the sunshine. Thank you for reading! I hope you enjoy this book and learn something new to help get you outside and on the water.

For Mom, Dad, & Steph

TABLE OF CONTENTS

Belonging in the Wilderness	3
About the Author – Amanda Marie	5
Preface	11
Stories On the Fly: It Begins with Water	15
Standing on the Bank: A Truth About Water	21
Standing on the Bank: A Truth About Women in Fly Fishing	23
Stories On the Fly: Learning, Re-Learning, and Learning Again	25
Standing on the Bank: Rods, Reels, and the Whole Dang Thing	31
Standing on the Bank: Casting and a Whole Mess of…Bugs?	41
Stories On the Fly: Matriarchs and Firsts on the Water	51
Standing in the River: Take a Sweater…or Don't	57
Standing in the River: What are We Even Looking At?	67
Stories on the Fly: New Water Everywhere	73
Standing in the River: That's All Great and Everything, But Now What?	79

Kneeling in the River: The Sacredness of Wild Spaces   85

Stories on the Fly: Nope. Not an Expert.   91

Breaking the Bubble Line: Creating Spaces of Belonging   93

A Final Note for My Guys: 97

Acknowledgements   99

PREFACE

Boys do it; how hard can it be?

It's the social media mantra that has flooded all spaces, from the blue-collar to C-suite. As women we are not unfamiliar with the feeling of being present in a male-dominated space. On the river with my fly rod tucked up underneath my arm, a silken thread in my fingers, a tiny fly in my palm I am still in that space. But unlike any other space, I am here for me. I can close my eyes and hear the steady flow of water over multicolored rocks. I can smell the wet green that saturates and gives life to the banks. I can feel the crisp mountain air that trips and tumbles through the trees above me. This is the feeling of being centered. This is the grounding that brings me back to feeling like myself, with nothing to prove to anyone. I am constantly chasing this feeling. I know I'm not the only one.

I've spent so much of my fly fishing career navigating spaces where I was the only woman in the room, never mind being the only brown woman in the room. I handled these spaces by leaning into my shy and soft-spoken nature to protect this small piece of belonging that was created for me by my father. I was fortunate to have someone create that space for me as a child and recognizing this, I was terrified of failure. Failure meant disappointment to the people who brought me to this space. Furthermore, to fail publicly in a room where I was the only brown woman is to damage or worse, lose that belonging. There is a lot to unpack there, but that's for another book. In the outdoor industry, the secret to men's success is that they're not afraid of failure. They don't need to be afraid of failure because they have claimed their permanent belonging for themselves in the wilderness. We need to do the same, and so I wrote this book for you.

You're the girl who has scrolled your phone on lunch break looking at all of the beautiful places women are going and those beautiful things women are doing and creating. The one who thinks it would be neat one day to say she's traveled to that tropical place and experienced great things. The one who has eaten fresh fruit cut from a wide-leafed tree in the jungle. The girl who has trekked through the dust and rock wilderness and knows the crisp feel of a mountain lake beneath her fingers. If you take nothing else from this book, even if you decide not to fly fish, I want you to know there is a space for you out there. You belong in that grove of century old trees. The thick scent of old-growth moss, ferns, and life filling your lungs. You belong on that sand flat with more shades of ocean blue than you imagined could exist. The warm water of the sea on your skin, and the thick green of the mangroves cutting the horizon. Standing in the water with a fly rod, this is the view. These are the places we come to reconnect with that space inside of us. That part of us that belongs in the wilderness. You come from an ancient line of women who were caretakers of the soil and stewards of the waterways. Their histories might be lost to you, but the connection still stands. The connection is soul deep. You belong to the soil and these waters. You were made for them.

This power in water and in nature is accessible simply by being present. The wilderness doesn't care about who you are, what your degree is, or how much of a "productive member of society" you are. It cares that you are observant and focused on what is in front of you. It's this focus that is centering. It reminds you that you are alive. In a world where we are constantly jumping from one thing to the next in a sterilized environment, the focus this kind of experience provides is an unmatched cleansing of the soul.

STORIES ON THE FLY: IT BEGINS WITH WATER

Water leaves a mark wherever it goes. The trenches, mountains, and valleys of the llano estacado, mesas, plateaus, and canyons are evidence of its will. The landscape of the desert is a testament to the history of the earth and its relationship with water. With every new torrent of rain and layer of sand compressed by wind and gravity new chapters of that history are uncovered. In the desert life thrives by making the most of the rain it receives. This truth is the heart of my relationship with water and fishing: making the most of the moments I am gifted.

    I grew up on the central coast of California in a place that was commonly mistaken with the Central Valley and the capital of California, that not-so-small canyon between the pacific mountains and the central plains. In my grandparent's age this valley was dominated by the agriculture of orchards, fields, and vineyards. The air in the summer would be filled with the thick spices of pepper, garlic, eucalyptus, oak, and alfalfa. This rich earth and fragrant air filled my childhood with an idyllic space for connection to nature I know now I was privileged to experience.

Living away from that space for so long has left me with a sense of longing for things I took for granted. One of those things being fresh fruit. In the summer during the harvest, my mom would take my sister and I to get fresh *fresas* – strawberries – from the fruit stand a mile away from our house. We would drive with the windows down in the heat of the summer. The worn fabric of the car's upholstery was rough against my bare legs. The hot breeze from the pepper fields we drove passed was spiced and sharp in my lungs and on my tongue. I could close my eyes and feel the heat radiating from the pavement of the road, and then the immediate cool rush of air as we drove by the fields that had just been watered. My sister and I would follow our mom out of the car once we reached the fruit stand. The summer immediately wrapping a warm blanket around us without the breeze. Speaking Spanish to the man running the stand, mom would pick out the baskets she wanted. With a smile the man would bag the baskets, and cut up a fresh slice of watermelon or honeydew for my sister and I. With flushed embarrassed faces and sweaty hands, my sister and I would thank him in English.

These were my summers as a child. My days revolving around the fresh fruit abundantly available at every street corner. I made sure that my showers were short and cold to conserve water so the farmers could continue to feed us all the delicious things we loved through the season. At least, that's what my mom and dad told me. Water is precious, scarce, and scared. It's not to be wasted. My parents were always outside. There was always something to do that was in nature whether it be working, fishing, hunting, gardening, or just being. For all of my childhood and well into adulthood they encouraged me to be and do the same. I can call my parents and relay to them frustrations and difficulties, and my mom will still say: Maybe you should go for a walk. Growing up this suggestion would irritate me to no end, so I would always end up sitting or lying down underneath a pepper tree in the backyard, and listen to the wind tumble through its willow-like branches and then skip through the leaves of the poplar trees nearby.

"If you listen really close," my mom would say "the wind can sound like water." As an adult it's the sound of a breeze skipping through leaves that centers me. It sounds like a creek or small stream in the desert. It sounds like home.

My father worked in construction with his own excavation business. My mother worked for UPS when I was little until she stopped working to focus on my sister and I. We went to a small public school exactly two miles away from our house. Then, because of my father's income and the building growth in Silicon Valley we went to private school a 45-minute bus ride away. In our free time as a family, we were outside. We got up before the sun on weekends and drove hours just to be on the water or in the mountains looking for water. As a child, fishing was boring. I hated it. I liked fish, but the waiting around was annoying. It was being outside I loved.

I didn't realize how much being in nature and around water shaped me until I moved to New Mexico as an adult. I was accepted into the University of New Mexico for a master's program in Rhetoric and Writing, and when I had visited the campus with my mom, and never felt more like a stranger in my own skin. I was surrounded by warm, sun-kissed terracotta buildings, mountains that turned a blushed pink in the sunset, and wide blue sky that left no where to hide from the sun. This was my mom's dream, and I was living it for the both of us. As a student she had completed some community college, and now at that same age I was going to start my second degree. I felt unworthy and awkward, and I was hundreds of miles separated from the ocean and water to heal my unsteadiness. I chose the University of New Mexico not only for its program, but because half of my family originates in Carlsbad. Living in Albuquerque for over two years was a kind of reckoning for me, and it was also an awakening to my connection to water. The air in the desert and in the shadow of the Sandia Mountains doesn't wrap you in a warm blanket. It scorches with heat or cold and burns with wind or dust. When it rains, it downpours, rumbles, and flashes. It rips the heavens open with a power that molds the earth with artist's fingers. It is terrifying and beautiful. The reconnection with my own history and this land would be the same.

Water is powerful. The desert landscape is carved by floods. There is a stretch of highway between Roswell and Carlsbad where the desert flatland is intimidating. There is no cool green to break up the heat of the paved road, there were no fruit stands with *fresas* and corn and honeydew. The air is heavy with the scent of desert clay, mesquite, and sage. There is no water. There wouldn't be water until it rained. There are no trees to hide from the unforgiving sun. This is where my ancestors first carved their existence. I understood why they chose to travel: if they didn't, they wouldn't survive.

We all have family stories that are told with a biased lens of time and nostalgia. Many of our stories were about my grandfather, my mother's father, working as a cowboy. But the realities of his life were far from rose-colored, and coming to this desert re-affirmed my family's histories, but not in the way I had imagined. Instead of seeing the romantic beauty of land I was told about, I was confronted with the reality of survival as a difficult battle. A battle that would leave my grandfather's bones broken and skin leathered by the wind, heat, cold, and sun.

There is a picture my mom has of her father. He is seated in the saddle atop a tall black horse, dressed in a black cowboy hat, dark button-down shirt, reigns of the horse held loosely in his hands. He looks like he was born to be seated right where he is. A king on his throne. I imagine him this way when my *abuelita* fell in love with him. According to family legend they ran away together, my grandfather spiriting her away from raising her ten siblings to live on a ranch with him where he worked. Of course, this may or may not be true, but it's the story nevertheless. One thing is for certain: My grandmother claimed she never really understood what he did for a living until she came to live on the ranch with him.

As she tells it, she woke up one morning because there was a commotion outside. People were yelling, and whooping, and cheering. It was early in the morning, and she didn't understand what all the noise was about. She got out of bed and put on her robe and a sweater, her long, hip-length black hair braided and pinned up. She went to the back door of the small house where they lived and peered out to the pastures where the horses were kept. One small pasture she could see was the source of the commotion. And there he was, her new husband, seated squarely and fluidly on the back of a horse that looked like it was trying *de matarlo* to murder him. What was worse, the men standing or leaning on the fence of the small pasture were egging him on in his pursuit to ride this wild animal. My grandmother screamed. She had just married this man and now he was going to be killed by this stupid horse and leave her alone at this ranch with all of these strange men. She screamed again. Somehow, my grandfather heard her. He turned in the saddle and easily dismounted from the bucking horse. He climbed the fence to the pasture and swung down from the rails, hitting the ground running towards her and their small house.

"*Mi amor, que paso?*" he asked. *My love, what's happened?* His dark eyes looking around for danger and finding none, and her own astonished expression taking in his confused one. In my grandmother's story she politely demands an explanation for what exactly he was doing riding that horse that clearly didn't want to be ridden, and whether his intention was to make her a widow within the first week of their marriage. He laughed at this. I can see his wholehearted smile and the lines crinkle in the nutmeg skin around his eyes, and I can see my grandmother fold her arms across her chest and frown in the most displeased expression known to man.

"*Mi amor, es mi trabajo,*" he would say. *My love, this is my job.* His kind expression would make her angrier because how dare he scare her like that, and didn't he know better. Eventually, he would explain his work on the ranch and show her their new home: a working cattle ranch, in the desert, and close to water.

I come from a history of people living intimately with the land. My ancestors were ranchers, farmers, cultivators, holistic healers, and foragers. They understood the balance needed between being harvesters and caretakers of the earth. It's this delicate balance and dance I come home to every time I step into a river. It's my place of healing and reconnecting to the earth as a sacred space. It's a celebration with my ancestors and loved ones that we've finally made it to where we were going; we've finally come home to water.

STANDING ON THE BANK: A TRUTH ABOUT WATER

The very nature of fly fishing comes from the use of artificial flies used to catch fish. These flies are meant to imitate the type of food fish like to eat, and it's these tiny flies, tied onto nearly invisible line, and flown through the air with remarkable grace, that make up the media's perception of fly fishing. Now, I'm not going to lie to you and say that fly fishing is for everyone. It's not. Fly fishing is challenging. I have spent hundreds of dollars on a week-long vacation and ended up sitting on my ass crying on a river bank. I have experienced the lowest of lows and the highest of highs in the same day while out on the water. So why do it?

Put simply, it's a perfect mirror to life in its abundance. Fly fishing is joy, anticipation, puzzle, heartbreak, triumph, the richness of learning cultures, and the experience of new and old relationships. It is all of this while being irrevocably tied to the curative power of water.

When you talk to guides and listen to people who have been doing this for decades, they all say the same thing: It forces you to be present. Fly fishing isn't something you can do while also doing five other things. The river and the water and the fish demand your full attention. You can't be thinking about what you're going to make for lunch, or how you're going to deal with traffic, or overanalyzing that presentation you made, or wondering if you ever actually pressed send on that email. No, you're forced to be in the moment and fully focused on the task in front of you. You're forced to put down your phone and read the water or find the fish you're going to make your next cast to. There is a connection that is made when confronting a challenge in the wilderness. For men it's a conquest; read most books about exploration or fishing written by men and the undercurrent is always conquest. But the experience of fly fishing is so much more than that: It's a puzzle box or a maze that is equally beautiful, frustrating, and exhilarating. It's a challenge that requires technique instead of brute force. We are not so powerful that we can bend Mother Nature to our will, but if we can observe and listen long enough, we might be able to join her in her dance. It's this delicate dance that's the most exhilarating experience I've ever known.

To help you understand, I want you to do a small exercise in meditation. Think about a moment that excited you. But not just any exciting moment. I want you to think of that moment where you felt the excitement in the pit of your stomach, or in the flutter in your chest. You were so excited that your brain couldn't fully register what was actually happening. All of your other senses were overloaded with that moment and nothing else in the world existed. Then, when the moment passed, you were left in awe. Before you open your eyes, sit in that moment, that feeling of awe.

That's what it feels like each and every time I bring a fish to the net or to my hands. Awed into speechlessness. That's the moment we are always chasing.

STANDING ON THE BANK: A TRUTH ABOUT WOMEN IN FLY FISHING

We're better at it. That's right, I said it.

I'm not the only one who has said this. Pick up any article written by a fly fishing guide or instructor and they will tell you the exact same thing. Women who start fly fishing are there to learn, to be at peace in nature, and to have fun. Men who start fly fishing are mostly there because of ego. Egos get in the way when it comes to fly fishing because it's as much a mental sport as it is a technical one. As an angler, you are first and foremost at the whims of Mother Nature. The surest thing to happen to an overconfident ego when heading out on the water is less-than-ideal weather conditions, technical difficulties, and non-existent fish. So, naturally, women tend to be more successful, learn faster, and get more enjoyment out of the experience than their male counterparts on the water.

More importantly, casting a fly rod is all about timing and technique, and the more you try to muscle through it, the worse your casting is going to be. In its simplest form, casting a fly rod relies on the laws of physics and has nothing to do with how strong your arms are. Casting and reading the water are all a puzzle, and the beauty of that puzzle won't come to life if it's smashed into oblivion to force the pieces to match.

Everyone comes to this sport in their own way, whether it's through a book, movie, friend, or family member. We are captivated by the artistic beauty of it. Fly fishing looks effortless. The settings are always peaceful and idyllic. It looks like the angler is painting the sky, and if it is a painting, you belong in that painting. Your presence is not going to mess it up, not going to be a burden to the landscape. You belong in a place of peace. Sure, there is a learning curve, but don't be fooled into giving up. Don't be intimidated. You're going to be better at fly fishing in the beginning than most men who start in the sport, but it's certainly not all going to be rainbows and sunsets. You're going to fuck up and end up in a mess of line, and that's okay. We all do. It won't be the first time and it won't be the last. The point is, you'll still be out there on the water. You'll still have a great adventure to tell and experiences to share. You'll still be in that painting.

One of the most important concepts fly fishing leans on is observation. As women, we have spent our entire lives perfecting this skill. We've studied how people interact in a space and used those observations to help us and others be successful. It's why many of us are educators, caretakers, doctors, and lawyers. That's not to say that men are not observant they are but women are different in that many of us have been culturally conditioned to be quietly observant and in the background almost all of our lives. These are the skills fly fishing requires. The most successful anglers are the ones who carefully listen to the space around them, observe what is happening in the water before them, and make each moment count.

STORIES ON THE FLY: LEARNING, RE-LEARNING, AND LEARNING AGAIN

I was introduced to fishing by the man the world gifted me: my dad. I know not everyone is so lucky or privileged. It is my greatest hope that by the end of this book, you'll have found or be inspired to find those people who will support you like the ones who have supported me.

Both my sister and I have pictures as little ones of wild hair and colorful clothes, silly expressions on our faces standing next to a stringer of fish or a singular fish that is as big as we are. My mom is always behind the camera, and my dad is always next to us kneeling on the ground or in the boat. That is how we grew up. Road trips in the car, going to the lake, camping, fishing all day, making hotdogs, and eating potato chips. My mom making us food and packing lunches, and my dad driving the boat and securing our life jackets as he helped us aboard. All of my favorite memories are out on the water, kissed by the sun or the breeze and sung to sleep by the slap of water against the hull of a boat. They are tinged with the smell of old plastic Robo-worms and the funky feeling a new plastic Brush-Hog leaves on your fingers. These memories are of the excitement and wonder of a fish flopping into the boat, checking on them in the live well and giving them names. Then, releasing slimy shimmery bodies back into the water and watching them disappear into the green-blue depths wondering what it would be like to follow them. My parents were there every step of the way. They told us the names of the different types of fish and how to tell them apart. My dad constantly educated us on how fast or slow to reel in our bait or a fish, and my mom was always behind the camera making sure we would have pictures to share and look back on one day.

I was introduced to *fly* fishing by the man I chose for myself: my partner. We came into fly fishing together as kids-trying-to-be-adults, building our new lives together in the desert and on the water. He was a boy and I was a girl, and together we had really big dreams of adventures we had yet to build and experience.

I was on an airplane flying from Albuquerque, New Mexico to San Jose, California. I was seated next to a guy in his late 40s, and like the socially awkward shy person I am, I struggled to keep up a conversation with a male stranger. We had talked about golf, and then I told him how my partner was getting into fly fishing. I remember saying that it seemed cool, but I didn't know if I could get into it. Fly fishing seemed too hard, too beautiful. It was too full of mystery, experience, and wisdom. It was a sport for Hemingway or for older men who had experienced life. It was a sport for all those grandfathers who had built their fortunes. I was a young klutzy girl who stumbled through life because people thought she was cute, and that was my only saving grace. I was a grad student living on a stipend with enough savings to get me a plane ticket back to my parents for a visit. I had dreams of being a writer and writing about deep soul-changing things, but I hadn't experienced enough life yet to know what those things were. How could I take up an art that only the wiser, older, male "elite" participated in? Would doing so be disrespectful? Could I even afford it? And how would I learn? Wouldn't I be a burden to those others who are more experienced than me?

This kind guy in the seat next to me on the airplane looked at me and said "Well, he's in love with you now and you already know how to fish. He's going to love you even more if you learn how to fly fish."

Of course, looking back now at my silly-girl self from a growth mindset, this is a prime example of what supporting a culture of toxic masculinity looks like. Women learn this skill so a boy will love you and work to support you. I can see my feminist fairy godmother rolling her eyes and crossing her arms with a rolling pin in hands. She's going to smack him first, but then she's going to smack me.

Of course, my early-twenties-self took what this stranger said to heart. My entrenched fear of inadequacy took over and said, "Girl, you better learn how to fly fish so you can make your man proud of you and he'll stick around." And so of course I took up fly fishing! Of course I agreed to my partner teaching me! Of course my learning process involved fights, arguments, temper tantrums (on my part), and the loss of a ton of flies!

After one particularly big fight on the river, I stomped off to a field to practice my casting alone and to seriously reconsider the wisdom of taking advice from a stranger on a plane. What made me even more angry was that I was starting to enjoy this stupid fly-fishing thing. I wanted to be good at it for myself and not just for this boy I fell in love with, this boy who I was witnessing every day and with every challenge, grow and change, evolve into the incredible person I know him now to be. I was falling in love with the long days on the river. The sun on my face. Me, this girl who grew up naively sheltered by the quintessential California sunshine was being shaped into the woman I am now. The woman I continue striving to be.

Together we are irrevocably changed by the sunsets over the water and the experiences of trekking up a river with your best friend, the smiles and laughs shared over a particularly dramatic fight with a fish. The nights next to a campfire where we've faced our demons together, and met the sunrise with kinder hearts and a deeper understanding of ourselves. The ghosts of generational trauma, and the men and women we were fighting to become. The partnership we've built together as we've grown from our challenges and triumphs is something I still cherish every time we set foot in a river. These are experiences and adventures that fed my soul. This was the type of life and relationship I had always dreamed about: One that was built by growing and evolving and fighting for our dreams together.

But I wasn't getting this whole fly fishing thing, and it made me angry and mad and frustrated and humiliated. For some reason I kept making the same mistake over and over again with each cast, so much so that fixing it in that moment became impossible because I was too angry and tired of failing.

I would like to say that I no longer have days that I feel like this, but it would be a lie. I would also like to say that the more experienced fly anglers I have talked to - the people who have been doing this for years and/or decades - also no longer have days where they feel like this. But it would also be a lie.

Fly fishing is hard. As women we are not immune to the hard things. We are intimately familiar with the challenges of being in these difficult spaces. Sometimes it sucks. Fly fishing is using the laws of physics to make magic while holding a stick in your hand. It's some kind of fucked up simple sorcery that works, and when it works right and all of the pieces fall into place you can catch a fish. The difference is our ability as women to see and notice and appreciate those moments of growth as they happen. Like witnessing a child try something new, fail, fail again, and then learn, adjust, and succeed. Again, this isn't to say that men are incapable of being just as observant, but only to say that as women we have been conditioned to notice, observe, and carefully react, because in many cases our lives, careers, and safety have depended on it. Why not take that hard-learned skill of observation, diligence, and careful persistence to heal and bring peace? Because when the connection is finally made, and I catch a fish, it's that same feeling I had as a child: watching in wonder as this powerful glittering creature disappears into the depths of the abyss. Only now I am experiencing this in a life not built for me by my mom and dad, but by me and my man and the life we have created together.

In case you were wondering – yes. It's worth every second.

STANDING ON THE BANK: RODS, REELS, AND THE WHOLE DANG THING

Like any sport, fly fishing can be as expensive as you want it to be. It can also be as inexpensive as you need it to be if you're willing to use your resources to help get you started. This is where it is important to find your local community of fly-fishing women. I guarantee they have all the gear, all the knowledge, all the experience, and they are more than happy to share with you what you need to get you started.

A FLY ROD AND REEL

Please don't do your retail therapy at the beginning of a new hobby. Take it from someone who has done it before with almost all of her hobbies, and now has too many unfinished projects. If you live in the United States, consumerism is real, marketing is on-point, and we all have that side of us that loves the serotonin rush of buying something new. Don't do it with a fly rod and reel set up before you've even attempted a cast. Go try out a casting clinic before you spend your hard-earned money.

Now that that's out of the way, here's what you need to know:

Fly rods are categorized by a weight system. The bigger the number the sturdier the rod. If you're going to go for something really fast or strong, such as a sword fish or marlin, you're going to use a heavier rod like a 12 weight. If you're going to fish for baby trout under twelve inches, you could probably get away with something like a 3 weight rod. The weight of the rod you choose to use will also depend on the types of flies you are using. Casting a dry fly with a 12 weight is nearly impossible the fly is too light and the rod is too sturdy, so it's harder to "load" the rod (more on what that means later), and therefore harder to cast and get the fly where you want it to be. A 6 weight rod matched with a 6 weight reel is probably going to be your best friend in the beginning.

There are also different rod lengths. These vary from six feet to fourteen feet. If you're just getting started, you don't need anything excessive. A nine foot rod will help you get comfortable with the basics of casting and line management. A nine feet might seem excessive but trust me, it's not. It's the most common length of fly rod made, and appropriate for the most common situations in which you'll find yourself when you're first learning.

Finally, fly rods are made up of lots of different materials including bamboo, fiberglass, graphite, carbon fiber, or some combination thereof. My personal suggestion is going to be to start out with a graphite/carbon fiber rod. They're popular, easy to use, and mostly affordable on the second-hand or previous-year model market. With a little research, you can find what you need to get you out on the water within your budget. You don't need to spend thousands of dollars to be a part of this community and be successful and enjoy it.

A few things to look for when you're going to buy secondhand:

1. Make sure there are no big scratches, nicks, or scrapes.
2. Look for any cracks where the pieces of the rod are joined together.
3. Make sure the guides or eyes of the rod aren't bent, chipped, or cracked.
4. Make sure the reel rotates smoothly and that the drag works.
5. Make sure nothing is bent or severely scraped.

Again, don't purchase any of this until you've met up with a group of women and taken a casting class. They will have more specifics for you and will help you out when looking for secondhand gear to start you on your adventure.

Okay, so a 6 weight rod matched with a 6 weight reel will get you just about anywhere, fishing all types of water, for all types of fish, and with most types of flies.

Now, notice I mentioned matching a reel that is in the same weight category as the rod. This is optimal. Remember I said casting a fly rod is mostly about using physics and learning technique? The right reel will appropriately balance out the weight of the rod. This will make it easier to cast and use the laws of physics in your favor. Reels are intentionally matched with their corresponding fly rod weight. If the reel is too heavy for the rod, you'll feel like you need to muscle-through the cast. This will make your casting worse. Guaranteed.

The best way I can explain the importance of a balanced rod/reel combination is using a scene from *Pirates of the Caribbean*. In the beginning the blacksmith boy is presenting the governor with a special sword he smithed for the new commodore's promotion ceremony. He unsheathes the sword and balances it on his fingers. The sword remains perfectly balanced between the weight of the hilt and the blade itself. It's perfect.

Take aways: Jack Turner was a heartthrob according to my younger and not-so-younger self. Also, the more balanced the sword the easier it is to wield. Likewise, the more balanced the rod and reel combination the easier it is to cast and the more badass you'll look and feel out on water. Remember: You belong in that painting. Even when you fall on your face in the river, you still belong in those beautiful places.

BACKING & FLY LINE

There are a million different fly lines for a million different purposes. For now, it's best to be as simple as possible.

The first type of line that goes onto the reel is the *backing*. Backing is often thinner than fly line and sometimes has an almost fabric-like feel. It helps the fly line sit better on the reel, and gives you extra length in case the fly line itself isn't enough. Backing comes in all different weights and colors, and isn't anything terribly precise. There are different strengths for backing like there are different strengths for fly line, but most fly shops will probably recommend 20lb strength - or *test* - and anywhere from 150 to 200 yards of backing itself. Ultimately, pick a backing that suits you and use it. Better yet, let the fly shop you visit pick it and put it on the reel for you. Many fly shops will help you get set up this way if you have a reel and are purchasing fly line from them already. When you get into more advanced fishing, you can get into the nitty gritty of backing, but for now, all you need to know is to have, use it, and make sure it's still in good working order at the end of each season.

Most fly lines are a type of *floating line*, meaning the line is hollow on the inside and will float accordingly. When you're first starting out, you'll want a floating line that matches your rod and reel weight. This is the line you'll actually be casting, so to recap, so far, we have a 6 weight rod and a 6 weight reel, and now we want a 6 weight line.

Fly line is both stronger and more delicate than you think. Try your best not to step on it or crush it in any way, remembering that it's hollow inside. This line has been specifically engineered by people way smarter than I am to accomplish two things: float and cast. Floating becomes very difficult if the hollow space on the inside of the fly line has been crushed or punctured, and casting becomes very difficult if the fly line is nicked, crimped, or simply is no longer hollow inside. Fly line also has memory. It spends much of its life coiled around a reel or on a spool from the factory, so if you find your fly line keeps tightly coiling up on itself when you cast, it might need to be stretched. You can do this by heating up the line through friction between your fingers. Pinch the line firmly between your pointer finger and thumb and carefully stretch it out on the spaces where it is coiling. Doing this a few times will help the line release that memory. Ironically, the tension created from catching a fish will also help to do the same.

Every fly angler has the brand of fly line they prefer. Read the reviews and ask your new community what they recommend. In the end, you'll find the one you like and will probably stick with it forever. Then you can become a brand ambassador and you'll be on a beach with your margarita in no time. Just kidding! Results may vary.

LEADER AND TIPPET

The next two kinds of line are *leader* and *tippet*. The leader is the line that attaches to the end of your fly line, and the tippet attaches to the end of the leader; the fly itself will attach to the end of the tippet. The difference between the tippet and the leader is the tapering of the line. Leaders are often tapered, meaning the diameter of the line gets smaller as it gets to the end. The thickest end is used to attach to the fly line, while the thinnest end is used to attached to the tippet.

The tippet has the same diameter and weight strength throughout. It's used at the end of the leader for a few purposes: First, it's meant to be invisible in the water so that the fly at the end looks like the most natural thing in the world to the fish, and it's hard to do that when the line being used is clearly visible in the water. Fish are almost always smarter than you think they are.

The other purpose is to save the leader in case something catastrophic happens. Catastrophes can range from casting into a tree, casting into your fishing partner, the rocks, yourself, a dog, or any other obstacle that happens to be in the way. The tippet will break off instead of the more valuable leader or fly line. Consider it a safety net for the inevitable time you'll need it. Of course, if any of these things were to happen and the tippet does its job and breaks, you are still going to lose the fly. Take that for what you will.

There are as many different types of leaders and tippet as there are different types of fly line. As a rule, it's easiest to start with a tapered leader that matches the weight of your rod/reel/fly line combination. However, know that this will change depending on the type of fly you're using and fish you're targeting. Not every fish needs a tapered leader. Not every fly needs tippet. Some fish are particularly toothy and will need steel leader, while other fish might be too big and strong for the tippet you've chosen and will break it in a matter of seconds. And even still there are some situations where it doesn't matter what you're fishing for or what you have tied on, your leader will break simply from the fish's sheer force of will. And if you go down the rabbit hole and choose to adopt this sport as one of the things that brings you joy, you will probably end up making your own leaders and using tippet only when it's expressly necessary.

Despite these many permutations, match the rod/reel/fly line combination for your leaders and tippet until you're told differently by that group of women who are quickly becoming your new best friends on the water.

PUTTING IT ALL TOGETHER

We have backing, fly line, leader, tippet, and potentially a fly someone has given you. You have to put it all together somehow. Great! This is the order they go in when you're setting up your rod, reel, and line.

The backing for the reel should come first and be set up before you even get out on the water. As mentioned before, some fly shops will be willing to walk you through the steps, or even do it for you. If you're doing it yourself, tie the backing on the inside of the reel itself with a simple knot before you start spooling it on. This knot doesn't need to be anything fancy; it's just to hold the line in place before you start spooling it on. The backing should fill up to a quarter inch from the top edge of the reel itself. It's okay to get out a tape measure if you need it.

Once the backing is evenly on the reel, the next step is to add the fly line. The fly line should be tied to the backing via an *Albright knot* or a loop. This makes a seamless connection between the backing and the fly line. I've chosen to leave the description of this knot out of the chapter because it's one of those knots you will probably never have to tie yourself, and one that the nice folks at the fly shop will do for you. If you need to switch fly line off your reel for whatever reason, you'll simply be spooling it off, backing and all, onto a paper towel tube or other cylinder, and taking your reel in to be re-spooled with a different line by the nice people at the fly shop. You're a beginner. It's okay.

But we will talk about other knots. Don't be intimidated - there are only three. You can practice them as much as you want from the comfort of your couch with a piece of paracord or yarn, and you can watch as many videos on them as you need to help things click. Learning these three knots will not only make you more self-sufficient on the water, but you'll also be able to help your fishing buddy when they need an extra hand. I've included some basic images in this chapter to help give you a basic understanding of what these knots look like but you'll want to practice them as much as possible on your own to be comfortable with them.

First is the *perfection loop*. This is the knot you'll use to connect the leader to the fly line and is the least-frequently-used knot out of the three. I mention it first because it is often the last one people learn, but the first one they need when something catastrophic happens to their leader. If you know the perfection loop it will make you feel a whole lot better about whatever disaster just occurred and will help get you back out on the water that much sooner. Once you've created your perfection loop with your leader, you'll want to thread the loop through the pre-made loop in the fly line itself. This loop is heat-treated and seamlessly a part of the fly line, so you don't need to worry about creating a knot in your fly line to connect to your leader. Now that the loop is through the one on the fly line, thread the tail end of the leader through the loop itself. Pull tight and seat the connection you've just made, making sure there are no spaces left and all of the lines of your knot are aligned and touching. By the end of the process, you should have something that looks like the picture below.

The second knot in the system is called the *triple surgeon's knot*. This knot connects the leader and the tippet together. It's the second-hardest because it's connecting two independent lines together to create a seamless straight line. The better this knot is the easier it will be to control how the fly will move on the water, and thus it's important to have this knot be as seamless as possible. Any type of current or movement will cause the knot to disturb the water, and potentially distract the fish from where you want it to be focused on. This is also the knot that connects the invisible line to the fly, so, it needs to be as delicate as possible. Finally, this knot needs moisture to be seated correctly. This means it needs to be a little wet when being pulled tight for the first time. Most anglers accomplish this by either putting the line in the water or in their mouth. Your choice. When you're done with the triple surgeon's knot, it should look something like this:

Finally, the last one in the system is the *clinch knot*. This is the knot you'll use every day, sometimes multiple times a day, when you're out on the water. It ties the fly onto the end of the tippet. It's important to also make *this* knot as seamless as possible because it is the strong connection point between you and fish you're going to catch. There will be a time when you lose a fish because this knot fails, and it will be heartbreaking. It will be the catalyst to taking this knot seriously. Practice it as much as possible, and you'll be glad you did when you're out on the water and need to change flies on your own. This knot also needs moisture to be seated correctly. Do what you will to make that happen. When you're done with the clinch knot, it should look something like this:

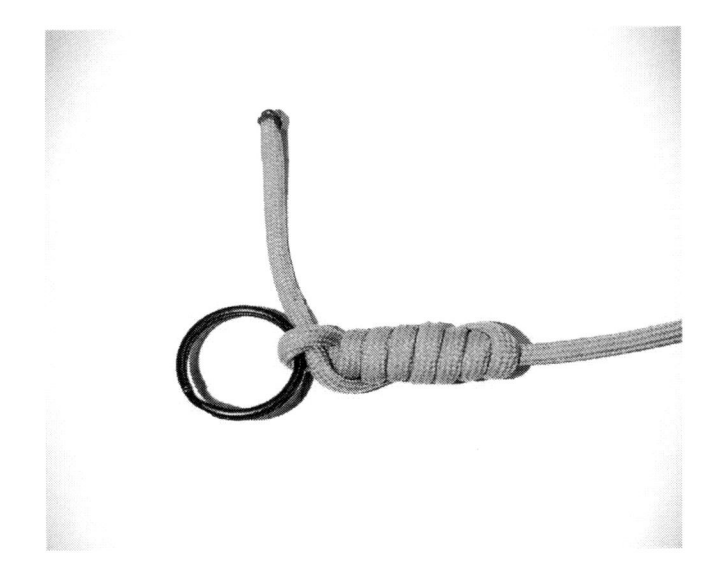

STANDING ON THE BANK: CASTING AND A WHOLE MESS OF...BUGS?

FLY CASTING

Notice how we haven't talked about flies yet? That's on purpose. It's a whole thing, and you're not there yet.

When you are first starting out and learning to cast, tie a piece of fabric or yarn to the end of your tippet or leader. It will mimic the weight of a fly just fine and it won't get too caught up on anything to damage your borrowed or new-to-you fly rod set up.

I'm not going to pretend to be able to teach you how to cast a fly rod from this book. I can tell you the basics of how it works, but it's not a technique you can learn by reading about it. You have to see it, do it for yourself, and practice it in person. This is one of the spaces where your new community will help you the most. Make no mistake, casting is half the battle when it comes to fly fishing. It's also one of the things that makes the experience so special. Take some time at a park, on lawn, or in a field to practice and learn your cast.

As I mentioned before, the fundamental concept of casting a fly rod is based in physics and technique. Unlike conventional fishing gear, you are physically using the fly rod to move the line, and in turn to launch the fly to where you want it to go. Conventional gear relies on the tension already created by the reel to help sling the lure or bait out to its destination.

In fly fishing, *you* are the one who is creating that tension for casting by bending or *loading,* the rod. This happens by moving your forearm and the rod so the rod tip is pointed behind you at 2 o'clock and stopping, then bringing the rod tip forward until it is pointed at 10 o'clock and stopping. This movement will cause the line to fly behind you and bend the rod towards you. When you bring the rod tip forward and stop at 10 o'clock, the line will fly forward because the rod tip is flicking the line in that direction. If you point the rod tip back behind you a second time at 2 o'clock, the rod tip will repeat the process, bend, and flick the line back behind you. The bend you're creating in the fly rod is called *loading the rod*. All you really need to know: Loading the rod is your best friend.

And if absolutely none of that made sense, trust the process. Sign up for that casting class. Learn the technique. Don't muscle through it. You'll do beautifully.

FLIES

Did you know that there is a whole group of grown-ass men who make a living doing arts and crafts?

Go to a fly fishing or fly-tying expo, and you will see miles upon miles of thread, feathers, sparkle, glitter glue, special curing lights, beads, and furs. Still don't believe me? Look up fly tying supplies online, or visit a local fly shop and witness their materials wall. I've been fly fishing for over six years now, and it still fascinates me that these men will spend this much money on materials and time to create these tiny little things. And some of them have a problem with women scrapbooking? Seriously? I digress.

I've left the art of flies and fly tying for last because aside from learning to cast, learning the types of flies and techniques to fish them can be some of the most intimidating information to learn. Science has told us that the insect world includes about a million different known species that only represent about ten to twenty percent of the actual estimated number of insect species in existence. Fly anglers have not even scraped the surface of that number of different types of flies, but I am willing to bet they have tried to get to at least a fraction..

Fly tying is an art in and of itself. If you choose to dive into this sport head-first, fly tying will be something you will consider making a part of your new hobby. But as fun as it would be to buy all of those new craft supplies and a kit to get you fly tying, that's not why we are here. We are here for the basics. No, you don't need to take up fly tying if you want to learn to fly fish. What you will need to learn are some basics about bugs and when to use them.

BUGS: THE BASICS

As mentioned in the beginning, fly fishing is named because the of the artificial flies used to catch fish. Picking out which type of fly to use to imitate fish food will depend on the species of fish being targeted, the time of year, temperature of the water, and whether or not Mercury is in the microwave. Ultimately, picking out which fly to use for which fish is a giant guessing game that everyone in the fly-fishing community will collectively pitch in on.

It is also important to know that the term *fly* does not indicate "insect" in all instances. A "fly" can imitate anything from a bird to an insect larva. It can also imitate things that don't exist in the natural world and are simply meant to be big and flashy. In the end, if you can imagine it, a fly has been created in its likeness.

I am going to assume you are new to this community if you have made it this far into the book. I am also going to assume that you do not have a degree in entomology. Good news, friend! I also do not have a degree in entomology. It's not necessary. What is helpful is knowing a few basics and some terminology. In the next few chapters I will review some common types of flies you'll find in a fly shop. This list is by no means definitive. As you progress in the community and meet more people, you'll learn about all different types of flies, their purposes, and the multitude of ways to fish them.

One last thing before we get started: sizes. The size of the fly is determined by the size of the hook. Traditionally, the larger the number the smaller the size of the hook. This means the larger the number, the smaller the size of the fly. I know, it breaks my brain too. It also means that some of us are on the cusp of needing glasses and will have a rude awakening when we try to tie a size 22 fly onto our nearly-invisible tippet. No, I don't need to be reminded. Yes, I have an appointment to see the eye-doctor. Leave me alone, Travis.

Mayflies

Mayflies are a major food source for trout and are typically what is shown when the media depicts fly fishermen. You've probably seen pictures of a man standing in a river with a chunky vest, waders, a fly rod, and a cloud of insects surrounding him. Those insects are probably mayflies.

The great thing about fly fishing is that you're dealing with artificial insects on the end of your line, so there is no need to get your hands smelly pinching worms or hooking on live bait. The downside is that you may end up in the middle of a *hatch* at some point in your fly fishing adventures. This just means you could have hundreds of thousands of insects flying around your face and getting stuck to you.

If I haven't lost you yet, and you didn't just throw the book across the room, congratulations! You're braver than I was when I first started. If you are now recovering from the fact that you just chucked a book across the room at the mention of tiny insects being stuck to you, don't worry. The odds of this happening for you as a beginner are rare. The important thing to know is that mayflies are at the bottom of the food pyramid for trout; they're often the foundation on which everything else is built.

Mayflies have an interesting life cycle that starts underwater. They spend most of their lives nestled in the rocks and substrate as larvae. When the time is right according to the season, temperature of the water, and barometric pressure, they will emerge to molt. This is when they shed their creepy alien-like exoskeleton and transform into winged adults. They live in the air and above the water for an extremely short period of time (one or two days), and then they die. Their sole purpose for living while they have wings is to mate and lay eggs. Unfortunately for them, they're cheeseburgers for trout. Fortunately for us, they don't bite or sting.

If you are fishing for trout, selecting mayflies for your fly box means you should try to have flies that imitate the different lifecycle stages. These include flies that both float on top of the water, and ones that sink or sit just below the surface of the water. These flies are made of all types of material, but the most common include synthetics, feathers, or elk hair.

Now, don't get out your credit card just yet! The process of selecting flies shouldn't happen in a vacuum. Ask your new community of women for their advice. Make it a coffee date to go to a fly shop and learn about their selection. Take a class on fly tying where all the materials are already provided and learn about the different flies. Watch videos online about different flies and their purposes. Do. Your. Research. None of us have the endless stream of income available to simply show up at a fly shop and purchase all of the things. You wouldn't be reading this book if you did. There are thousands of different types of bugs, and depending on the season, geographic location, you may be looking at different types of species of mayfly in your region. Lean into your community to help you figure out what works for the water you're fishing during the time of year you are going to be fishing it.

Caddisflies

Caddisflies are the boring brown cousins to the mayfly. They are practical and purposeful. Unlike the mayfly, caddisflies undergo a complete metamorphosis from egg, to larva, to pupa, to adult. They also collect things in their larva case-making stage to create a little shelter for themselves as they grow. Things that often stick to them in this stage are mostly pebbles and bark.

At the end of the day caddisflies are simply another type of bug that trout love to eat at all stages of their development. They also participate in a hatch much like the mayfly. Similarly, the available flies for the caddis pattern range anywhere from imitating the egg and larva to the winged adult stage. One of the most popular caddisfly patterns is the elk hair caddis which is considered a *dry fly*. A dry fly is a type of fly pattern meant to sit on the surface of the water. Another term you'll come across is a *nymph* fly pattern (more about this in a bit). A nymph pattern is meant to sit just below the surface of the water or at different levels in the water column depending on how heavy they are. These nymph fly patterns are meant to imitate several different types of insects in their larva form, and are usually used in conjunction with a second fly that sits on top of the water. If it sounds like it's complicated, it's not. All you need to know for now is that nymphs are below the surface of the water, dry flies are on top of it.

The media has a tendency to lump all people who fly fish into the category of *dry fly* fishermen. This is like saying all people who wear makeup know how to contour. Have we secretly tried it? Yes. Are we good at it? Probably not. Do we do it all of the time? Definitely not.

Stoneflies

Stoneflies are creepy alien-like creatures. For real. They're weird. They also come from an ancient line of bugs as old or older than the crocodile and can grow up to three inches long in their full adult stage. The best thing about stoneflies is they are clumsy. No need to make a perfect cast where the fly gently floats through the air and barely disturbs the water when it lands. Nope! Stoneflies often meet their demise by getting the attention of fish because they've fallen out of a tree and made a nice *thwack* on the surface of the water. That means when trying to imitate an actual stonefly, it's okay and sometimes even encouraged to make a little noise when getting the fly in front of the fish. This simple fact can make stoneflies sometimes easier to use than the feather light caddis or mayfly.

Midges

Midges are tiny insects that are the bread and butter of fly fishing, and often used by beginners in their nymph form. Fishing with midges in their nymph form is like using worms: It's almost always successful if done correctly, and it's not very difficult. There is a wealth of great articles online that can tell you exactly how to fish this type of fly and the variations you can use. A few things to know about midges are they have a life cycle similar to the caddisfly, but they usually expire quickly in the emerging phase (i.e., when they are shedding their larval exoskeleton to transform into their winged image). This is because midges shed their larvae form while on the surface of the water instead of crawling to a rock or tree for assistance. This is incredible in and of itself, but it also gets them gobbled up very quickly by fish who watch them flopping around on the surface of the water and only want to help.

Nymphs

Nymphs are meant to mimic the larva stage of any of the bugs described so far in this chapter. Nymph fly patters can range from uncomfortably tiny to just a little bit larger. The important thing to know about nymph patters is they are not considered a dry fly pattern because they do not sit on the surface of the water. The nymph is special in that it can be weighted any number of ways to float, sink, or stay suspended in the water column. Fish are constantly moving vertically and horizontally in the water column depending on the current, temperature, and where food is being funneled. The fact that these flies are meant to do the same depending on how heavy they are makes fishing with nymphs very productive. Most trout will eat nymphs on most days because nymphs are bugs in the larva stage, and that's a trout's bread and butter.

Nymphs are also commonly fished below an *indicator* of some sort. An indicator is what the rest of the fishing world would call a bobber, but it's not necessarily the white and red stripped plastic ball you're thinking of. An indicator can be anything that sits on top of the water and floating downstream of the nymph tied on to the end of the fly line. This floating object can be a bigger dry fly, a small ball, or a piece of sticky foam. As long as it floats on top of the water and downstream of the nymph bouncing along the riverbed or suspended in the water column behind it, it's doing its job. The angler's job is to watch the indicator and set the hook when it gets pulled underwater by either a rock, a tree, or a fish.

Not all nymphs are fished below an indicator, however there is a very popular style of fishing known as *Euro nymphing or Czech nymphing* where no indicator is used at all. This type of fly fishing is very different from western flyfishing and requires its own setup and gear. It's techniques and artistry could fill an entire book on its own, and are outside the scope of this one.

Streamers
Streamers are a type of fly designed to move as much water as a fish does when it's swimming, and in most cases are meant to imitate the colors and patterns of small fish. Streamers don't always look like fish though. Sometimes they're big, flashy, and flirtatious because they can be. Sometimes they catch fish, and sometimes they don't.

Streamers are fun and can be exciting to fish because the goal is to imitate another fish or creature in the water. It becomes more of a game of imitating how a crab would float or crawl across the sand, or how a fish would flee from a predator. Because of this, streamers are often used when fishing for more predatory fish, who are hunting other creatures rather than slurping up bugs in large quantities. In most cases this makes predatory fish more aggressive, and the more aggressive they are the more fun it is to experience connecting with them. Now, I'm not saying catching a fish on a dry fly is boring. Far from it! But catching a fish on a streamer is 110% a new and different experience all its own.

Beads
Fishing with beads is most commonly practiced in Alaska and it means exactly what it sounds like. There are whole companies who make a business of buying and coloring beads to look like fish eggs. These beads come in all different colors, sizes, and textures depending on what type of fish egg they are imitating. Beads can be mottled, milky, spotted, opaque, clear, or any combination thereof. When salmon are spawning in the river, their eggs will look different depending on how

old they are or where they are in the fertilization process. These beads are meant to imitate those many stages in a similar way that nymphs are meant to imitate various types of insects in their larval stage.

Beads are fished much like nymphs. They're suspended on the leader line above a bare hook and behind a floating indicator. The indicator will float down the river and let the bead bounce along the bottom of the riverbed behind it, and it will disappear under the surface of the water when the hook becomes caught on a rock or eaten by a fish. As I mentioned in the beginning of this section, beads are predominantly used in Alaska, and as a result may have different rules around them depending on the area you're fishing. The reason this style is so popular in Alaska is because of the migratory salmon runs that happen five to six months out of the year, when rivers can be flooded with so many salmon eggs that it distorts the clarity of the water. That's why it's only natural that the fish living in these rivers eat the eggs as a source of food instead of relying solely on insects.

It's important to note that state and regional regulations on the use of beads change depending on where you are and the river system you're fishing. It's always important to review the regulations on the river you're planning to fish before heading out on the water. When in doubt, ask your local fish and wildlife office to clarify.

STORIES ON THE FLY: MATRIARCHS AND FIRSTS ON THE WATER

When I was a child, fly fishing was something my father did visiting his cousin in Montana. It was shrouded in mystery and the solitude of the great outdoors. My view of the community has come a long way since then. I had been fly fishing for five years when my partner and I moved to Alaska, and it was another year after that until I would fly fish with my father for the first time.

I'll never forget standing in the river next to him, the glacier topped mountains reaching up to the sky behind us. The water at our boots was crystal clear, enough to see the gravel bed below our feet and all its colorful rocks. He has been taking me fishing all my life, but this time it was my turn to take him.

My partner and I had a year to explore our new home before they came to visit, and I knew exactly where I wanted to take them: the Kenai River, Valdez, Girdwood, Whittier, and Seward. I knew they would love all of it. This is how we grew up: traveling, seeing the world, fishing, and hiking. My parents both grew up in the central coast of

California. They moved a few times during their relationship, but never outside of the county and never after myself or my sister were born. They lived in the same house they bought when they first got married, and only recently sold it some thirty years later. Even though we never moved, my parents made it a point to take us on road trips every summer and school break. We would go into the mountains or desert. We would fish and build campfires. We would cook and nap in the shade or by lantern light. These childhood memories were my inspiration for our plans for their first Alaska adventure.

We met my parents at the airport. I saw my mom's smile. I gave her a hug. I was home. Sometimes that's all it takes.

The first time we floated a river with my parents was in Idaho. We were in paddle boats, and my mom was seated in an oar boat following behind us. This trip down the Kenai would be much different: We would all be together in one boat and not in whitewater.

The Kenai is one of the most popular guided rivers in Alaska. It gives everything you imagine Alaska would showcase for a river: blue glacier water, deep, beautiful pools, panoramic views, and vibrant fish. The first half of the float from the bridge was scenic. The water was deep and slow coming out of the lake. It gave us time to orient ourselves to the grandeur around us, and to teach my mom and dad how to bead fish with a fly rod. They're quick learners, so they caught on easily. My dad told us all he wanted was "for Mom to catch fish." It was because like everyone who has spent time with her, he was addicted to her smile and her laugh. It's wholehearted. It's all in or nothing. It's infectious.

The first spot we stopped to fish was full of sockeye salmon staging to make their way up the river. My partner oared us into the eddy and dropped the anchor. Dad and I got out to fish upstream and my partner instructed mom to fish the school in front of the raft. He tied on a pink streamer we'd had success with before and walked her through targeting fish. After a few casts and losses, she hooked into a sockeye and the world lit up.

A few minutes later, Dad hooked into a chum salmon, and my partner was able to net it just as it started to rain. Their first salmon on the fly accomplished.

The next weekend we made the trek to Valdez after work on Friday. I called ahead and reserved our favorite camp spot and was so excited I could barely contain myself. This would be it: the true Alaska experience for my parents. Camping on a mountain, under a full moon, and in beautiful weather. The drive to Valdez follows the Copper River and showcases miles of waterfalls that betray the nearly rainforest-like climate of the region. Valdez itself sees an average rainfall of around seventy inches per year and is surrounded by green, glacier-carved mountains. The dramatic presence of these mountains is overwhelming. So much of these mountains are untouched because of their vastness, and that night our campsite showcased the best of these views. From our spot on the mountain, we could see two glaciers across the canyon that stretched before us and down to the town, and up the canyon as far as the eye could see were untouched ridgelines of green. We made dinner over the fire and watched the sun dip below the ancient mountains. We shared hot coco and stories and marveled at the galaxies that spun out across the inky purple sky. We made plans for the next day's fishing and adventures and went to bed with full hearts.

The next day, we were out on the river fishing the clear streams for one of our favorite kinds of fish: Dolly Varden. These fish are mostly silver and come with all different types of colored spots and stripes, from champagne to the richest emerald, and they put on a dramatic show when you connect with them. They're known for their jumps, twirls, and enthusiastic flops which make them a lot of fun on a fly rod.

WooHoo! Mom's voice echoed over the water. I turned around from my spot in the river next to my dad to see. My partner was reeling in his line and walk-running down the bank to my mom calling instructions:

"Get to your reel! Point your rod towards me!"

She was laughing and giggling, bending her fly rod in a rainbow arch, and reeling in her fifth Dolly Varden of the day. My dad laughed. My partner pulled his net from his pack and mom swung her fish to him. She quickly released it back to the crystal blue water and marveled as it slipped through her fingers. She was smiling for days.

There's a picture that sits in my dad's office of him and my mom holding up two largemouth bass in their boat, and next to the picture is a plaque on the wall. They've been tournament bass fishing together since before I was born. It's more than the competition and the prizes for them; it's the community and the friends they've made. The experiences they've had together. This is what always brings them back to the water. It's what brings us to the water now in Alaska, and what will keep bringing us back time and time again no matter where we are.

White-tipped fins slipping effortlessly through weathered and sun-kissed skin. At the end of fishing season, we always hold our hands out to compare them. Tanned and freckled skin up to the cuff line, and then a stark contrast of color where our long sleeve shirts have protected us from the sun. We laugh because even though our hands are clean, they're browned by the sun. We wear sun gloves now as my parents get older and as our hands are exposed to different environments, but we still compare our hands at the end of each season, sometimes at the end of a great day of fishing. These hands briefly held beautiful fish. These hands held pieces of the rainbow. These hands that look like both my mom's and my dad's, have fumbled and been gentle, have been strong and not strong enough, and have tried again.

When we cared for my grandmother as she got older, I always took note of her hands. Even when her dementia progressed, I marveled at how her hands remembered to crochet patterns, smooth a tortilla, and braid our hair. My sister has her hands. Their shape and sturdiness. My mother's hands have their own color and lines. When my hands are dark after a season's worth of fishing, they wear the same sun-kissed olive brown. I know one day my hands will look like hers. I love that they will. Maybe because it means when they do, I will have tried to live for the quiet moments of persistence and love and peace like she has.

It's not enough to say that Mom is everything to our family. She is our matriarch, our blood, our bond to this world and our past. She is the peace that steadies us in the storm and the joy that celebrates with us at the mountain top. I can't wait to share our next adventure together. Maybe I'll learn a little more about how I can grow up to be like her. All I know for certain is, I am endlessly thankful and humbled to call her mine.

Everyone remembers the first fish they landed on a fly rod. It's my greatest hope you get to make these types of memories with the ones you call friends and family.

STANDING IN THE RIVER: TAKE A SWEATER...OR DON'T

The best advice a fisherman ever gave me was to pack what I thought I wouldn't need, because it would be better to have it and not need it than to need it and not have it. That fisherman was my dad, and it was quickly followed up by my mom handing me two extra jackets and an extra pair of shoes as we walked out the door. In the same space of time, my mom would look me up and down and either give me the approving nod or the disapproving wide eyes of many a Latina mother who was silently admonishing her daughter for her choice of clothing.

Unlike my mother and my grandmother, I won't hand you an extra five layers and tell you to put on a sweater as you head out the door on your next fishing adventure. I will, however, tell you to connect with your new group of fishing friends and see if they have extra gear to try out before you spend your hard-earned dollars on your own. This sport, like many others, can be expensive. There is an economic barrier to this community, but there are also organizations out there dedicated to bringing people to the sport who are just like you. There are also quite a few things that are transferrable if you already have gear for hiking, backpacking, or other water sports.

That said, you'll want to make sure to gear up with a few things before you get on the water. First will be the clothing you're going to wear. This is going to depend on the environment you're fishing; the clothing recommended for an Alaskan river trip is going to be very different from what's recommended in the Carolinas. A few basics to keep in mind are layers, good socks, breathable pants (or leggings), sunglasses, bug protection, and a hat. All the clothing should be a type of breathable synthetic material or a blend of synthetics. Think workout clothes.

Why not your everyday cotton t-shirt? There is a saying in the outdoor rescue and safety community: cotton kills. It's true. If you're going to be sweating or anywhere near water, it's best to stay away from cotton. This material is absorbent and will cool you down. It does its job very well. The unfortunate part about cotton is it doesn't wick away sweat or humidity, it retains it. This can lead to a chill even when outside air temperatures are high. In short, you'll be cold and wet, which can lead to hypothermia if you are outdoors for an extended period of time. And yes, people can become hypothermic even in the middle of summer. The goal is to be safe and have fun! We don't have time for hypothermia.

The synthetic workout-type clothes are going to be your base layer. Depending on the location being fished and the weather, bring other layers that can withstand being wet. These can be things like a fleece pull over, synthetic puffy jacket, and/or a waterproof rain jacket. Personally, I always get cold. I am also fishing in Alaska. I have layers upon layers and a sweater when I'm out on an adventure. Mentally, my grandmother is still shoving an extra jacket in my hand as I run out the front door.

SUN PROTECTION

I know the struggle. I grew up in California. Everyone was tan or trying to be tan, and it was the standard of beauty. You know what we're all regretting as we enter into our thirties and forties? Sun damage.

The important thing to know about sun protection when out on the water is that it also pertains to your eyes. Not only do sunglasses protect you from the rays being reflected off the water, but they're going to help you actually see into the water. Polarized sunglasses are going to cut out the glare on the surface of the water and help you learn what to look for when you're fishing. Fish are camouflaged very well - their lives depend on it - so it will take you awhile to train your eye on what to look for when you're fishing, but eventually you'll get it. A sturdy pair of polarized sunglasses will help you get there. It will also keep you out on the water for longer and thus give you the chance for more adventures in a day.

Finally, sunscreen technology has come lightyears from when we were kids. It's no longer oily, thick, and sticky like mayonnaise. There are even companies that make reef safe sunscreen that doesn't harm the environment you're enjoying. Wear it.

WADERS & WADING BOOTS: WHAT ARE THEY ABOUT?

There's a reason I've put off this topic: It's the second most expensive barrier to entry new beginners come up against, and it also tends to be the thing people jump into buying right from the start which then sit in a closet unused. Lean into your community for this. Ask around for waders and boots you can borrow and try out before buying your own or look for discounted waders and boots in online spaces.

And depending on the type of water you're fishing, and where your adventure takes you, you might not need waders at all! There are plenty of people who *wet wade*. This means wearing sandals, or a neoprene sock with water shoes, boots, or good traction tennis shoes, and clothing that can get wet and drip dries easily. You'll see people doing this in the summertime or in climates where it is warm year-round. Anywhere in the continental United States where it gets hot enough to be in shorts or a skirt, you can wet wade.

There are two general categories for waders: Gore-Tex and neoprene. Which type of wader makes sense for you will depend on the type of water being fished and the climate. Gore-Tex waders don't have any insulation, and thus are not warm by themselves. They're simply a waterproof, windproof shell. This means those layers I mentioned earlier will be important to providing insulation to keep warm. Neoprene waders, on the other hand, come with built in insulation. They're thicker and often heavier than Gore-Tex, but because of this, they insulate very well without the extra layers, Neoprene also doesn't allow for much breathability as a result.

When selecting which type of material will work best for you, think about what you wear when you go out for a semi-strenuous walk or hike. Is the clothing breathable? Do you sweat or chafe? How is your temperature? Are you hot, warm, or cold? Most professional guides choose Gore-Tex waders because of their versatility. They're living in their waders every day and in all types of weather, so they need something that will function with whatever additional layers they choose to wear that day. Take their approach! The more comfortable you are out on the water, the more time you'll be willing to spend chasing fish, casting, and exploring. Think of those backup flats you keep stashed when you go for a night out on the town, or the comfy sandals you change into after a long hike. Why have them? Because they allow you to stay out later and keep having fun. If you're comfortable from the start, you'll be much more willing to stay out and keep adventuring.

Waders also come with different styles regarding their footwear. Some have integrated boots that are attached to the whole garment themselves, and some have a neoprene stocking foot that serves as a thick waterproof sock and is mean to fit into a pair of wading boots purchased separately. The difficulty with the integrated boot style of wader is the fit. Not everyone can comfortably fit in the one-size-fits-most boot that is pre-attached to the rest of the waders. Many people, especially women, are built with disproportionate foot to hip to chest ratios that many mainstream manufacturers still can't figure out. Keep in mind what you're going to be the most comfortable in. For an entire day out on the water, most people benefit from the stocking foot wader because they can easily find a separate set of wading boots that will fit comfortably and fits them better than a pre-sized pre-attached boot combination.

There are two basic types of wading boots available if you decide to go the stocking foot route: rubber-soled and felt-soled. Felt-soled wading boots are not allowed in all states or all waterways. For example, they're not allowed to be used at all in the state of Alaska, and the reason for this is because microorganisms can get trapped in the felt and be unknowingly transported from one river system to the next. This increases the chances of those microorganisms being introduced into a new river system they were never meant to be in. For all of my non-biologists out there, introducing new microorganisms into places they're not supposed to be is very bad. At its worst, it can lead to contamination of the waterway and death of the native fish we are all trying to enjoy and protect.

The most popular type of wading boot is rubber-soled. These boots are easy to clean, don't track microorganisms around once they are cleaned, and allow for more durability and longevity. The biggest thing to keep in mind with wading boots is that like any good set of hiking boots, they need to be broken in to become most comfortable.

The industry is getting better at making a wider selection of wading boots for women, but at the end of the day our options are still limited. The best thing to do to help pick your wading boot is to try them on with the waders you're considering buying. This way, it's easier to gauge how the neoprene booty fits with the boot itself and whatever sock you're wearing as a base layer. The wading boot will often be a bigger size that what you typically wear because there's simply more material around your foot when you're wearing it.

Once you have the waders and wading boots that fit you, take care of them! Always clean the boots and gear you've worn out on the water with mild biodegradable soap at the end of the day, especially if traveling between states and water-ways. It's important to leave all of those microorganisms where they belong and to not transport them to other places where they don't. No one likes to be abducted by aliens and then never put back in their home. Keeping your boots and waders clean also makes the gear you've spent your hard-earned money on last longer.

Fly fishing was not meant to be a sport or community for women, and I have never seen this more clearly than when I started looking for my own set of waders and boots. I distinctly remember walking into a fly shop in Idaho with my partner and being really intimidated and embarrassed by the meager selection of options I had as a female coming into this sport. We were standing on the second-floor loft of the fly shop and there was one set of women's waders on one wall and another set of women's waders on the opposite wall, and that was it. It was 2016. The variety and availability of gear specifically made for women has come light-years since then, but there is still progress to be made. Pick up any book at the library or book store about fly fishing and it's probably written by, and contains images of, white men. Look at videos online and in magazines and articles: men. I didn't have female mentors when coming into this space. It's my greatest hope that this book can lead you and inspire you to connect with yours.

There are organizations and people who are trying to change the image and reality in the outdoor space, but there are still limited options for women in fly fishing, and this includes with respect to gear like waders made in sizes appropriate for women. Know that when you go to a fly shop you may only see one or two types of waders marketed specifically towards women, but don't be discouraged. It's not you, it's the industry. Try everything on and ask all of the questions. Get your sizes and measurements and write them down so you can keep them, shop, and make the best decision for your body type. At the end of the day, comfort is key. Waders are going to be the thing you're going to spend all day in the rain, wind, sun, snow, and through all types of water. They'll keep you safe from things that poke and stab, bugs, and keep you warm and dry during all of your adventures.

NOTE ABOUT FLY SHOPS

Use the community as a resource. Going into a fly shop solo for the first time is intimidating. In an industry dominated by men, a female walking into a fly shop can be like a female walking into an auto parts store. It can be awkward, frustrating, and discouraging depending on the culture of the space. Find someone in that casting class you took to go with you. Reach out to any of the local women's fly fishing communities. Also, know that when you are asked about what size and weight you are, it's not from a place of shame. Outfitters ask these questions because they need to know what recommendations to make for you that will be the most comfortable and help you succeed in your adventures. The more comfortable you are, the more you'll be willing to brave the weather and other discouraging elements that can come along with the sport. Be honest! It doesn't matter how heavy or light, tall or short, or what your goals are. I was one of those girls who got criticized for being too thin and not eating enough every time I visited a grandparent's house. Contrary to every grandparent's belief, this feedback didn't make me eat more at the dinner table or make me feel more comfortable about my body. The fly shop isn't yours or my grandparents' house. Be honest with your measurements and numbers, so you can be comfortable and feel like a badass on the water. Finally, if you don't feel welcome, find somewhere else to support. There is enough negativity in the world without you having to wade through it to get out on the water to enjoy your peace and quiet.

A FINAL NOTE ON GEAR

A pro tip from many of the guides I have worked with in the past: Have the appropriate gear for the largest fish in the system. Researching the place you're going to fish and asking questions will pay off when you're on the water. Ask about how big and what the size range is for the fish where you'll be. This doesn't mean you'll only be fishing for trophy-sized fish and won't be satisfied with anything less. No. As women, we're here to have fun and enjoy the outdoors. Sure, it would be great to catch a world-record fish, but that shouldn't be the driving factor of the adventure as a beginner. There are women anglers who are after that trophy fish, but you're not there yet.

The reason it's important to know the size range of fish in the system is so you can plan for the rod weight, line, and appropriate leader and tippet set up. Tackling a river where the fish are consistently ten pounds or more with a light 5 weight rod and gear is possible. But it's not necessary. It also puts unnecessary stress on the fish being caught because the gear is too light to bring the fish into the net quickly. It's also very likely the line, leader, and tippet will break because too much tension is being put on gear that's not meant for the job. This means leaving line, leader, tippet, and hooks in a river or worse in a fish to potentially cause more damage in the future. Doing a little bit of research and asking the questions will help avoid putting more pressure than necessary on the ecosystem and will make you better prepared for the adventure.

Hooks are the last item I'll mention in this section about gear. Barbless hooks for freshwater fishing will help both you and the fish in the long run. It will help you as an angler because you'll be able to get the hook out of the fish easier, thus releasing it more quickly. It will also help you when the inevitable happens and you hook yourself or a friend instead of a fish. We all do it. It's a rite of passage at this point. If it's with a barbless hook, you'll be fine. You'll have a nice story to go with the new piercing you got on your fly fishing trip to Mexico. If not, you'll still be fine, but it may require a skilled fishing partner's assistance or a trip to the ER depending on the situation. In the case where you don't have a barbless hook on your fly, it's fairly simple to pinch or smash down the barb to make it essentially barbless.

STANDING IN THE RIVER: WHAT ARE WE EVEN LOOKING AT?

I remember standing on the bank of the Klamath river in Northern California and watching the water tumbling over rocks, dipping under tree branches, and spilling into calm deep, calm pools of green and thinking how peaceful and pretty it all looked. It was like a painting with green willows lazily stretching over the water and creating ripples in their own shade that were swept downstream into the foam of a rapid. It was idyllic and beautiful and I remember thinking nothing of it other than that.

My partner and I went back to that same spot six years later, and it was still as idyllic and beautiful as I remember it. The landscape of the banks had changed a little because of the floods a few years before, and there were boulders in new places. The water carved its way around and over them in its endless flight to the ocean. This time the river was different not just because of the floods, but because I could tell the fish would be sitting behind a particular boulder on the far bank, or in the deep pool below the churning foam of the rapid, or they would be on the bubble line tailing from the eddy behind the big boulder on my side of the riverbank. I saw where I would need to put my boat if I were to run that rapid successfully. The beautiful willow stretched over the water? If I were in a boat floating down the river, I would want to stay as far away from that as possible.

Knowledge changes us and the way we look at the world. For better or for worse we notice and see things differently when we have lived experience or education about situations, we were previously naive to.

READING WATER

Rivers are always changing. Anything that is coming into constant contact with water will be in a continuous state of change. Because of this, no two sections of river are the same at any given time. The ability to stand in front of a stretch of water and be able to identify what is happening is helpful not only for finding fish, but also for keeping you safe if you decide to step into it.

A few vocabulary words that are helpful to know are *riffle*, *run*, and *pool*. These are all used to define certain characteristics of a stretch of water. A *riffle* is when the water is disturbed, where it bubbles and shimmers at the surface. This often indicates shallow water because the smooth surface of the water is running over rocks and being scrunched, tossed, and jostled around. This also often creates oxygenated water or bubbles. Bubbles are usually a good thing because the more oxygenated the water the easier it is for the fish to breathe. Often, fish and other aquatic creatures sit in the riffles because they are high in oxygen, and food is funneled like on a conveyor belt through the area. Sometimes it's easy to see this conveyor belt where a riffle turns into a run or a pool because it appears as a line of bubbles on the surface of the water. This is what's known as the *bubble line*. It often sits on the edge of an eddy where the current is swirling. Fish like to hang out in the eddies because the conveyor belt is pushing food to them without them having to chase it down. When in doubt, always fish the bubble line.

A *run* is a deeper channel that often comes before or after a riffle. These deeper channels function like highways for fish or other creatures because they allow them to move easily between riffles and pools. A run is even sometimes deep enough to have different currents at different depths. The water at the top of the water column just below the surface is often moving the fastest, and the speed of the current will slow down the closer you get to the bottom. The water making contact with the riverbed is always moving the slowest.

It's important to understand that the water is moving at different speeds at different depths because fish often look for the path of least resistance. Oh, don't we all? But really, who in their right mind is going to sit at the top of the water column just below the surface and feel like they're running a million miles an hour. It's a whole lot easier to meander lazily at the bottom of the riverbed. I know which one I'd sign up for.

A *pool* is a deep calm space in the river. Pools are usually some of the deepest parts of the river and are the easiest to point out. They are places for fish and other aquatic creatures to rest and hide. Think of all of those wildlife shows that depict salmon moving up a river. One of the most iconic Alaska images is a giant school of red colored fish just hanging out together and circling each other. Ninety percent of the time they are doing this in a deep pool on the river, resting for a while before they collectively make a big push up a waterfall or riffle to attain the next big pool. Now, just because pools are deep and calm, doesn't mean they don't have current. They still do, and the same rules still apply: The slowest current is at the bottom and the fastest is at the top just below the surface.

Being able to identify these three characteristics will get you a solid start on how to put the puzzle together to find fish, but it's also important to keep in mind *structure* and *bottom composition*. Fish can be predatory to other creatures in the river, but they are also prey to any number of creatures inside or outside of the water, and they don't have a lot of tools at their disposal to defend themselves besides their ability to hide. This is where knowing how to identify structure and bottom composition come in handy.

Structure simply means anything that creates a deep pool or good hiding place. These can be trees, bushes, large rocks, caves, or any combination of these. You'll want to identify these areas and then try to fish them as best you can. Doing this can result in a catastrophe like I mentioned in the previous chapters, so be prepared to lose a fly and/or need to re-tie. But it's worth it when you catch a fish you knew was hiding there under that tree.

Bottom composition means what the riverbed is made of. Is it sandy? Is it pebbly? Is it rocky? Is it grassy? All of these things will determine how fish interact with that particular stretch of river. If it's grassy enough they might hide in it and not necessarily need trees or other structures. On the other hand, if it's sandy or full of silt, fish might not stay there for very long because it's harder for them to breathe with the amount of silt in the water that gets kicked up by the current. If the bottom of the river is pebbly, it might be a good place for fish to spawn or lay their eggs. It also might be a good place for them to find food because larvae like to stick to and hide in the rocks.

Other factors that go into the puzzle of reading water include what the weather is doing, the temperature of the water, the time of day, and even water clarity. All of these aspects will influence what fish are doing in any given stretch of river. If the water is too hot, the fish will go to the deep pools because that's where the cooler water is, and because it also takes less energy to hang out at the bottom of a deep pool or in a lake than it does to struggle in shallow warm water. If the water is silty or dirty, fish usually congregate on the edges of the river where there is less current and clearer water.

Some fish species are also migratory, spending only parts of their lives in the river and other parts of their lives in the lake or the ocean. So, where you caught a fish a few weekends ago might not be where those fish are anymore. Everything in the river is in a constant state of movement. This is what makes the puzzle equal parts challenging and exciting.

The best advice I have ever received from any of my guides and the great men in my life was to observe. When you get to where you're going to fish, take some time to look at what the water is doing. Analyze the situation to make an educated guess instead of floundering around looking for a fish. Remember that it's a puzzle you get to put together. Take your time and enjoy it.

STORIES ON THE FLY: NEW WATER EVERYWHERE

Setting out on a journey of firsts is exciting and intimidating in a special kind of way. The journey through British Columbia on our move from Idaho to our new home in Alaska was a first, and something that intimidated me to my core. What if we didn't actually like living in Alaska? We were moving our entire lives to this place we had only ever spent a few days in, could it actually work? Is there even a Mexican market in Anchorage? How would I get ingredients to make tamales at Christmas? What added more to my anxiety was the fact that my parents were somewhat incredulous to the fact that we were actually moving to Alaska and leaving the continental United States for the foreseeable future. As people who had bled, sweat, and built their living in the same county in California for their whole lives, Alaska might as well be a different country entirely.

From this experience and from so many others in my life, I've learned that I will forever be a student of firsts. Driving the Cassiar highway through British Columbia and connecting through the Yukon and into eastern Alaska was a journey I don't know if I will ever do again, but I learned a lot from the doing. The first time I saw the Chugach range and realized this would be home, my heart stopped. It's a series of mountains along the Knik River that stretches along the coast for miles until it reaches Prince William Sound. The ridgelines are dramatic and cut by water and wind at unforgiving angles and shapes. In the summer, the foliage is thick and almost jungle-like in places. Every green place is teeming with so much life the air is thick with its pulse, and you can feel it in every breath. It's intimidatingly beautiful. I had hesitated at the chance to live in this magical place because of the fear of not belonging, but I've since learned that this place, much like any other place I've lived, is what I make of it. And that there is in fact a Mexican market in Anchorage that has everything I need for tamales at Christmas.

What surprised me the most about moving to Alaska is the connection to family and my history that I didn't expect to find. We made our big move during the 2020 pandemic, and because we couldn't have the typical housewarming party, I decided to learn more about my own family history in the hopes of bringing pieces of my ancestry into our new home. It was the year I built my first *ofrenda* – Day of the Dead altar – to welcome my ancestors into our new home. It was the year I made tamales for the first time with fewer than three people to help. It was the first time I took a good long look around and chose to acknowledge the fact that this new experience is something I had never done or dreamed of doing before, and I was going to be kind to myself about it. I needed to be kind to myself and accept the amount of learning it would take to make this place our new home.

The decision to be kind to myself and accept my own learning curve was magnified again when my partner and I decided to go somewhere warm in the wintertime to fish. This meant learning a new type of skill: saltwater fly fishing.

Saltwater fly fishing is different from freshwater because the fish are in a league of their own. Spend any time in an aquarium or watch a documentary on life in the ocean and you'll quickly realize that these fish come in all different sizes, shapes, and colors. They're also very fast and strong because they have to be. Saltwater in and of itself is also a very harsh environment compared to freshwater. The salinity is corrosive to gear and being out on the ocean and exposed to the elements can be exhausting. It also requires different fly fishing techniques for casting, leader and fly line set up, knots, flies, and clothing. Essentially learning everything about fly fishing all over again, from the beginning, including re-learning how to read water, and with a steep learning curve because the fish are so much stronger.

We decided our "somewhere warm" would be Belize. I brushed up on my Spanish after ten year hiatus, told my parents that if we were successful, we would all be going for a family vacation, and boarded a plane. The whole week we were fishing was forecast to be scattered rain showers from to a tropical storm sitting off the coast of Honduras, and with this rain came unpredictable wind and tough fishing conditions because we were such newbies to this whole experience. It's a good thing our guide was not a newbie.

The first morning of fishing our guide brought us to a turquoise expanse of water that was in such contrast to our home in Alaska it almost hurt. It was like coming out of a dark room to a bright sunlit day filled with vibrant shades of white and blue and green. The air was warm and humid. The sea water wasn't frigid and felt like bathwater on my fingers. For the first time in a long time, I scanned the water for signs of life and wasn't aware of what I was looking *for* or looking *at* except that the water was a beautiful clear crystal. I felt like I was on a different planet, and in complete wonder of every new feeling that bombarded my senses to near overload.

At this first spot passed a row of green mangroves, our guide poled our boat to what I could only see as a grey cloud in the crystal water. Turns out it was a school of bonefish no less than twice the size of the skiff we were standing in. My partner was on the front flat deck of the boat and at our guide's instruction he cast into the cloud and brought the fly back to the boat by *stripping* in the fly line by hand. Stripping means instead of reeling in the fly line, he was pulling it back through the guides of the rod by hand to let it rest at his feet. This movement made the streamer he was fishing jump and dart in the water like a wounded fish or shrimp. The connection was lightning fast. The bonefish swallowed the small streamer turned its head and sprinted through the water hundreds of yards away from the boat in the space of a heartbeat. The line my partner had collected at his feet flew through his fingers, through the guides of the fly rod and out into the crystal blue saltwater after the fish he was connected to. The line pulled out of the reel making it spin and fast enough to make it sing in a *whirr* as the fish kept swimming at lightning speed away from the boat. Eventually, when all of the fly line had been spun off of the reel and the chartreuse backing was now clearly visible, the fish slowed, and my partner started reeling it back to the boat.

But when the fish was close and my partner was ready for our guide to bring this beautiful creature into our hands, the bonefish decided it had other plans and repeated the process of swimming away at lighting speed. The line in the reel flew after it with a *whirr* until the fish decided it didn't want to run away anymore and let itself be reeled back to the boat. After what seemed like an eternity and more backing than either of us had seen in our lives, my partner and our guide brought this fish to hand for our small group to stare at in wonder. The fish's grey pyrite scales glittered like mirrors, tiny mouth, wide observant eyes, and hard muscled form that would put any body builder to shame. It was truly a creature to behold.

I couldn't top that. I smiled so much my face hurt. My partner swore up and down that he used up all of his luck and it was all downhill from here. Our guide chuckled and got back onto the polling platform. I stepped up on deck. More often than not, the important thing about new experiences is to be honest with yourself and others, be open and kind, and embrace the new experience for what it is: something you've never done before. I was well and fully in over my head, but I was going to give it all I had to witness that beautiful creature again.

STANDING IN THE RIVER: THAT'S ALL GREAT AND EVERYTHING, BUT NOW WHAT?

Connecting to a fish and getting that fish to hand are the parts of fly fishing that get your heart racing and make time stop. They can be the vivid moments that make core memories and are guaranteed to be the stories shared around the campfire, but they are also moments best shared with a fishing partner in the moment. This is another one of those times to rely on your community. Get out on the water with a fishing buddy or group of friends and work together. You can help net one another's fish, give instruction on obstacles in the river, help watch for dangers, and build your overall community of people who enjoy this sport with you.

Setting the hook is going to be different depending on the type of fish you are targeting and the type of fly you are using. *Setting the hook* simply means embedding the point of the hook into the cartilage of the fish's mouth. Doing so on a fish with a dry fly is as simple as picking up the tip of the fly rod, coming tight to the fish so the rod is bent like a rainbow, and holding that tension to keep the hook set in its mouth. One of the best things anglers can do to protect and care for the fish they are catching is become good at setting the hook so it happens exactly where it's meant to – in the cartilage tissue in the corner of the fish's mouth. Fish suffer the most damage when they are not held correctly, kept out of the water for too long, bounced or jostled heavily against rocks or trees, or hooked somewhere that isn't in their mouth (i.e., belly, back, tail, fins, etc.). All of these potentially damaging and fatal things can be eliminated completely by learning how to safely and ethically handle fish once they've been hooked. I'll make sure to discuss more on this a little later in the chapter.

Streamer fishing is a little different from dry fly fishing as we've discussed. By now, you know this because of the fly pattern being used and how it's fished, but setting the hook is also different. When dry fly fishing you can simply pick up the tip of the rod, come tight to the fish, and done! Streamer fishing involves what's called a *strip-set*.

In streamer fishing, you cast the fly out to where you want it and pulling it back to you via the fly line in short erratic bursts called *strips*. This way, you're collecting all of that line you just sent out across the river back to you, and you're making the streamer swim like a wounded fish. When a fish actually attacks the streamer, you still need to strip the line back to yourself, and reel in all of the line, to bring the fish into the net. However, in that instant when the fish actually attacks the streamer, the angler's job is to keep the rod tip pointed at the fish and do one solid strip on the line to embed the hook in the corner of the fish's mouth as fast as possible. Then, once the fish is hooked, pick up the tip of the rod to create a rainbow, and keep tension like described before. That quick solid strip to embed the hook while keeping the tip of the rod pointed at the fish is a strip-set.

Fishing with an indicator can be really helpful because it will tell you when to set the hook. When the indicator is floating downstream of the fly and it suddenly disappears, set the hook! It's that easy. But what does that look like? Setting the hook with an indicator means doing a *downstream* hook set. This means stripping in any slack and pointing the rod downstream to create immediate tension. Then, hold that tension as described before. To make this a little easier to remember, hooksets are always away from the fish's head and in the opposite direction of where the fish's head is pointed. This helps set the hook in the corner cartilage of the fish's mouth.

Now that you know how to set the hook, you'll need to get that fish to you and into a net. This process is called *landing* a fish. The important thing to know about this part of the process is to try to do it as quickly and efficiently as possible. Keep your rod tip up and use the cork of the rod as a fulcrum. All of the strength in the rod comes from the cork where your hand is gripped above the reel. Use this part of the rod to put *pressure* on the fish. Pressure simply means keeping tension in the line connected to the fish so that the fly rod is bent in a rainbow-like arch. The apex of this arch should be pointed directly away from the fish. Once you have pressure, the second step is to *get to your reel*. The process of getting to your reel means holding the fly line to the fly rod with your casting hand so you can keep tension on the line connected to the fish. Then reel in all of the extra fly line that is currently pooled around your feet and/or legs. Once all of the extra fly line is back up in the reel, you can let go of the fly line in your casting hand. This will let you hold tension with the reel instead of with your hand. For beginners, the key to not losing a fish that's been hooked is keeping tension in the line while bringing the fish to the net. The tension in the line is what keeps the hook in place, and without it, the hook has room to swivel and turn and thus come loose from its position.

Now what? All the extra line has been collected from around your feet and legs, and you're still connected to this fish. Great! Now let's get that fish into the net. Hopefully, you're fishing with a friend and depending on where your net person is, you'll either want to physically move towards them to get closer, or get the fish to them. In either case, keep tension, and reel in line with your free hand. Keep the apex of your rainbow pointed away from the fish at all times. Never point the rod in a straight line at the fish you're connected to. The fly will break off the tippet or leader every time.

Depending on the type of fish they might try to *run*. A run is when a fish decides it really doesn't appreciate you and literally makes a run to get as far away as it can as quickly as it can. Let it run! Use the rod and its fulcrum to keep tension, and let the fish take as much line as it wants. Keep the tension in your rainbow, reel line back to yourself when it starts to slow down. If you see where the fish is going and can safely make your way down the river bank to follow it, do it. You don't need to stay in once place. Follow your fish if you can. This might sound difficult, and it is, but it's worth it.

If you're still connected at this point, you've probably broken into a sweat of awe and hysteria and are ready to see what is actually at the end of the line. You got this. Land your fish! Use the reel to keep tension and *turn* the fish to your net person. *Turning* means pointing the apex of your rainbow towards where you want the fish to end up. This will swing the fish into the direction of the net. To make this easier: If the fish goes right, pull to the left. If the fish goes left, pull to the right.

Landing a fish quickly and efficiently will take practice. The exact technique will change depending on the fish and situation, but the basic movements and skills are the same. Now that you've landed this beautiful fish successfully, you'll want to do one of two things: keep it or release it. Regardless of which decision is made, it's important to keep the fish in the water while you make this determination. The fish has been working hard against you and keeping it in the water allows it to breathe. Imagine running a marathon and then coming to a stop and not being able to breathe.

Keeping or releasing a fish entirely depends on the type of fish, state regulations, and subsistence needs or wants. The questions surrounding keeping or releasing a fish should start first and foremost with the regulations for this fish in the location being fished. Is it legal to keep this fish? Often times to determine this, it's important to know the rules before you set out or keep them on hand for reference, take accurate measurements of the fish, and correctly identify its species and sex.

The fly fishing community culture as a whole is largely *catch-and-release*. This means 99.9% of the time fish are caught and released back into the water to live their lives. I'll get into some theories on why this is a little later, but it is an important cultural aspect to keep in mind when stepping into the community. Most people don't keep and eat the fish they catch. So if we want to release this fish successfully, we need to do a few things to make sure it continues to live its life once it disappears from our presence.

First, if you're going to handle the fish you just caught, make sure your hands are wet before touching it. Most fish have a thin mucous layer that covers their scales to protect them. Keeping your hands wet helps minimize the damage to this layer. Take a knee in the river someplace shallow, so that you can hold the fish over the water in case it flops out of your hands. You want to make sure if it falls, it doesn't have far to go before it's in the water again. You also want to make sure it's in a safe place away from rocks or trees if it does fall. Taking a knee in the river is a sacred part of this process for many anglers. You're leaving the banks we live our days on and meeting this creature in their space before we all go our separate ways. It's a hello and a goodbye all at once.

Once you're in a safe place and keeling in the water, grip the fish by the juncture where the tail begins. This is called *tailing* the fish. Doing this helps stop the fish from flopping around everywhere. Notice I said it would *help*. It doesn't always stop it entirely from flopping around everywhere. Then, cradle the fish's head and front fins in your other hand to maneuver it out of the net. Try not to squeeze too much behind its front fins or around its gills. This is where its heart is. Keep the fish in the water as much as possible during this process, so it can continue to breathe. Remember, it just ran the equivalent of a marathon. Best case scenario, the person who netted your fish is also taking pictures of you releasing your fish, but above everything else savor this moment. Be present. This is part of the magic. The fish is in the water, out of the net, and you're holding it in your hands. It could swim away at any moment, but for now it's magically suspended in your fingers. When it's ready, loosen your grip on its tail and let it go.

KNEELING IN THE RIVER: THE SACREDNESS OF WILD SPACES

The most perfect connection of a hook set I have experienced happened on a float trip on a remote river in Alaska. It was day four or five and I was standing on the front of our raft floating down the river through the tundra. Instead of the sweeping mountains of our home, this wide and lazy river flowed through mesa-like plateaus covered in thick spongy grasses. Unruly willows and berry bushes tangling in thick swaths of green that held the banks of the river silt together in masses of exposed root balls. I was fishing a dry fly that was meant to imitate a mouse. It had little black felt ears, whiskers, a brown rabbit fur tail, and a foam body that sat high on top of the water and moved across the surface just like I would imagine a mouse would swim. The boat was floating up on a calm pool with lanky willow branches hanging over the water. I remember thinking, if I were a fish, I would be hiding right there. I made the cast and it landed perfectly. Right where I wanted it to be. I twitched the fly once and then twice, it's rabbit-fur tail swirling with each twitch and making a little rippled wake on the surface of the water. Then my heart stopped. Everything happened like it was moving through molasses. From out of the green depths of the river the fish swam up to the fly, and without hesitation it swallowed it whole. Then it turned its head directly away from me, and came tight to my fly rod.

The process after the hook set was probably the least ideal situation I have ever experienced while fishing, and involved an escaped phone, rafts bumping into one another, urgently pulling the raft over on the side of the river to look for said Houdini phone, not getting a picture of the most beautiful rainbow trout I've seen in my life, and never finding the device that had all of our waypoints for the trip on it. All of this is to say, make sure you have more than one device with waypoints for your backcountry trip on them, take pictures with more than one camera, and know that shit always happens on the river. Take the lessons the river teaches you with a grain of salt, learn from them, be kind to yourself and others, and get back out there.

Connecting with beautiful and unique fish is a big part of what this experience is all about. Everyone comes to this community for their own reasons in one way or another. A big reason people stay in the community is not only for this experience and the adventure, but for the conservation and the relationships built on the river. This is all predicated on the fact that if we as a community want to continue to connect with these amazing creatures in these beautiful places, we need to be preserving, protecting, restoring, and educating the public about aquatic environments and resources. Collectively, we need to be stewards of the natural resources in our waterways so they can continue to thrive in abundance. The more relationships we build on the river, the more time we spend in these wild places, the more we can advocate together for their preservation.

The theory behind catch-and-release fishing is rooted in this concept of stewardship. Successfully releasing the fish back into the environment will allow it to reproduce and continue its natural life cycle. We want these fish to be here for the generations to come not only for the enjoyment of our children or nieces and nephews, but also to maintain the ecosystem that relies on these fish.

I have never seen this more starkly demonstrated than when I started fishing in Alaska. So much of the ecosystem and health of the rivers rely on the salmon. The salmon are a primary source of food for bears, birds, and other creatures in the rivers during the summer months, but their impact extends much further. The soil on the banks of the rivers is enriched by their bodies after they die, and their flesh in the river provides a continuous source of food even after their eggs have hatched. Even deeper is the cultural connection to the people who have lived in this land for millennia. Their seasons and cultural rhythm are molded and shaped by the salmon and the ecosystem that thrives because of them.

This type connection to natural resources isn't exclusive to Alaska. I remember learning about the sacredness of these resources as a little girl who grew up watching westerns with my grandmother in her *casita* in California. The house was no more than a thousand square feet and made of painted barn-red stucco. Its back up heat source was the heavy wood stove in the corner of the living room. I would curl up on the couch with a colorfully crocheted blanket a friend had made her. She would sit next to me smelling like crispy tortillas because that's what she made me when I stayed with her. Her chestnut weathered hands tangled in soft yarn as she crocheted her own blanket to exchange with the friend who had given her the one I was using.

I was too young to go to school, so my education came from her stories, my parent's stories, Hollywood, and *Sesame Street*. I didn't fall in love with books when I was little. I fell in love with stories. One I remember in particular involved images of buffalo on the plains of

Wyoming, their black and brown bodies a sea of inky spots on the green grass and extending as far as the eye could see. I was in awe. This little girl with big brown eyes, unruly mousy brown hair, and a toy horse clutched in her fingers. I was equally devastated when thirty minutes later in the film, a similar image of these majestic creatures appeared on the screen. This time their strong bodies had been stripped of their heavy protective hides and left where they had fallen. No harvest. Simply complete devastation and slaughter for miles. I remember looking to my grandmother who said simply "greed is ugly." Her fingers sunk deeper into the soft yarn, and she continued her diligent work on the blanket.

With each natural resource lost, there is also a part of the ecosystem that is forever changed. We know this to be so from evidence with the species that have gone extinct or are endangered. A few things we as anglers can do to make sure the fish we pursue continue to thrive are keeping them wet and being mindful of where and when we fish. There are usually state regulations protecting certain species in certain waterways and during certain times of year, so make sure you subscribe to the local fish and wildlife newsletters, social media, and publications throughout the year. Regulations often change from year to year, and sometimes from month to month. In the cases where there aren't regulations, best practices include limiting the time it takes to land the fish, keeping it in the water as much as possible, touching the fish as little as possible, avoiding the gills and gill plate, and releasing it back into its natural environment quickly.

Some of the hardest and most delicate fish to handle are the little ones under 10 inches. It's especially important to take care of them because they have so many predators to begin with. Some species, like trout in a warm freshwater environment, are extremely delicate no matter their size. In the heat of summer waterways in the lower elevations can become too warm, and freshwater species like trout become stressed in warm water because they simply aren't built for it. They're meant to thrive in cool to cold water. Warm water makes them sluggish, have less energy, eat less, and thus expire easily if they spend all of their energy at once. If you live in an environment that gets really hot in the summer, it's not a bad idea to carry a basic thermometer with you in your gear bag, so you can take the temperature of the water in the location you're fishing. This can help you make the educated decision on whether to fish or travel to somewhere cooler.

STORIES ON THE FLY: NOPE. NOT AN EXPERT.

My partner and I moved to Alaska because it checked all of our boxes as far as things we enjoy outside of our normal nine-to-five lives. When I tell people I live in Alaska, they immediately think I am living in a cabin in the woods somewhere with limited access to running water and no electricity. I promise it's much more boring than that, and the HOA in my neighborhood would disagree with me. What I am fortunate enough to have access to is the expanse of endless wilderness that is this state. It's wild and beautiful and feels untouched in so many ways. It's everything you imagine when you think of wilderness. It's a place that can't be fully explored in a single lifetime.

Spring in Alaska is a special kind of awakening that only happens in the northern most territories. It can be snowing one day and raining the next. There can be beautiful sunny days that look like summer, then there will be days that are mostly grey. Spring also means training and getting our bodies used to hauling around the backpacks we are going to be wearing all summer for backcountry trips, fishing mountain lakes, and hunting season. Hunting, has more in common with fly fishing than most people would think. They are ultimately both puzzles that it takes time, research, and commitment to master.

Almost every year my partner and I have gone bear hunting in the spring in the hopes to get a black bear. As of the publishing of this book, we haven't been successful yet. If you remember, we moved up in 2020. We have, however, walked a few hundred miles with our rifles and backpacks and seen country that "certainly isn't ugly" as we crest yet another ridgeline with no bears in sight. I know. You're thinking: How have you gone this long without getting a black bear? It's Alaska, aren't they everywhere?

Sure they are! I could make a laundry list of excuses as to why we have been unsuccessful thus far, but I would rather point out a very important thing I have learned from my hunting career: Just because you decide to dedicate time to a hobby doesn't mean you need to be successful or even really good at that hobby. The goal is the experience and the joy it brings you.

Yes, this sounds like the consolation prize given to a person who would have surely died by now if their life depended on hunting and gathering for their own survival. Yes. You would be correct. But I'd like to challenge you to think of fly fishing this way. You don't need to be an expert. The goal is the experience, joy, and connection in the adventure. There are thousands of men in the community who fly fish and are terrible at it. The difference is, they don't let the fact that they're terrible at it stop them from participating. They still go out and experience those once-in-a-lifetime trips. It's about the experience. It's about learning, having the adventure, and finding peace on the water. You belong out there just as much as they do. And whether we're good at fly fishing or not, we still all become little giggling kids when we land that fish, we've all been dreaming about. That joy and excitement is just as infectious. It's what continues to bring us back to the water.

BREAKING THE BUBBLE LINE: CREATING SPACES OF BELONGING

It's no secret that technology is evolving fast in our ever-expanding and ever-learning world. The fascinating thing about technology is its ability in many ways to be a mirror to ourselves, our societies, and the human condition. It has the ability, for better or worse, to reflect back what we decide to put into it. If asked for images, pictures, and stories of people fly fishing, the responses given by AI and search engines are still predominantly male. This isn't to say that female guides and representation in the sport is non-existent. Throughout the United States and Europe, there is a proud history of women who have made their living in this industry and share their knowledge and expertise abundantly. Yet when we ask the algorithm, the reflection given back to the user is still the same: white, upper class, and male.

It's this simple fact remains: Knowledge and representation are powerful. If you take nothing else away from this book, I want you to know you belong out here on the water and in the wilderness. For as long as our recent history can remember the narrative surrounding fly fishing and outdoor recreation has been dominated by the male voice and gaze. This patriarchal lens has left little room for women to see a place for themselves in these spaces. The wilderness is portrayed as too rugged, too demanding, and too scary. Women aren't cut out for the extremes of Mother Nature, or so the male voice would have us believe.

Fly fishing is about technique and physics more than brute strength. I venture to say the same goes for any outdoor adventure. Take the time to learn the skills and research. Be the one reviewing the regulations, looking up your next fishing spots on the map, or reading about rivers and the types of aquatic life they support. The adventure will take be that much more successful and enjoyable in the doing. The truth is Mother Nature doesn't care who or what you identify as. The wilderness will exist and continue to exist long after we are gone from this earth. Our only duty to the wilderness is to be responsible stewards and caretakers. What we can receive in return is beyond simply enjoying the scenery. It's healing.

The reason so many people come back to fly fishing and the river is because of the connection and sanctuary it provides. It's a place we can learn about ourselves, make meaningful connections with others, and heal from the trauma of our civilized experiences. There are countless stories from veterans and survivors who will tell you these waters are healing. It gets us out of our own heads and connects us, literally grounding us to the earth and its rhythms. As women, we are constantly making sure we are safe, heard, and productive. Being these things in the wilderness means being present and that's it. It needs nothing else but time and our presence.

In the very beginning of this book, I mentioned finding that community of women anglers to connect with and help you learn. Do this first. Not only because it is safest to go out with friends, but you'll also have someone to enjoy the experience with. Then, find your home waters. Do your research on waterways in your area, the state, and local laws involving them, and go explore! Find your happy place that's close enough to home that you can go to on a weekly basis to practice your skills and find your peace. Learn about the aquatic life in the water. What are the fish? What do they eat? Where do they hide? Where do they sunbathe? Sit on the banks and watch, observe, and try to put the puzzle together for this place you can call home. This place doesn't need to be the most idyllic in the world. It can be a pond, a canal, a lake, or a creek. As long as it's legal to fish there and it holds life, you can explore it. The point is to familiarize yourself with the waterways around you, understand the habitats, the creatures that call it home, and the ecosystem that supports it. Are there other channels that feed into this main channel? Where do those offshoots come from? Can fish and aquatic life travel from one place to the next? What are the predators? What is the availability of food and insect life? All of these questions are pieces of the puzzle that make up every waterway. The more you learn and observe, the better you'll be at understanding how the ecosystem works, and how to find fish. It's a challenge that will bring you closer to the environment and wilderness around you in a very grounding way.

This is deep work. Finding our peace while standing in a river, sharing stories with our adventure partners, and building experiences in a community of people connected to water is transformative work. Water carves the earth's canyons and shapes mountains with its persistent fingers. It can shape us as well. It has been curative and shaped me in ways nothing else has been able to. I struggled for years with uncertainty and awkwardness about who I was, where I came from, and how I got to where I am. We don't need to be Hemingway's or Fitzgerald's to be a part of the story. I don't come from a lineage of fly fishermen. I come from a line of people who were always in search of water to heal them and to rest. It's these people, their stories, and their cultures who have passed down that need for connection to the earth. A connection that has brought me to my peace. More than anything, I want you to know you can do the same.

A FINAL NOTE FOR MY GUYS:

I have been fortunate enough to have a community of amazing men in my life who have supported me a thousand percent in and outside the spaces where I was the only woman in the room or on the water. I am where I am today because they were willing to teach me without prejudice and out of genuine friendship. Being an ally means supporting without ulterior motives of a date, or anything outside of platonic friendship. These are your sisters and daughters out on the water. Support them and share the knowledge you've amassed so they can stay safe, comfortable, and succeed in their adventures. We all have a duty to do this above anything else.

ACKNOWLEDGEMENTS

I couldn't have written and chosen to publish this book without the support of my partner and friends and family. It has been my experience as a writer to write things and then store them away like a can of beans. Thank you, my love, for pushing me to share my words with the world. Thank you to my parents who instilled from the beginning the love of fishing and everything outdoors. Thank you to all of the good friends who were brave enough to read the first iterations of this book as beta readers and encourage my messy drafts. Thank you to my editor, Steven. You kindly helped me navigate my drafts into the finished product. For your patience and encouragement of my vision for the book, I am forever thankful. Thank you to my professional as-fuck photographer, Jess. You're an artist. Thank you for sharing and including me in your art. Thank you to my nine-to-five team. You've held space, taken an interest, and encouraged my life outside of the corporate world when you didn't need to. Finally, thank you to the many freelancing teams that have helped put this book together from cover art, formatting, and publishing advice and direction. Nothing happens in a vacuum, and it's the important work you do that makes it possible for writers like me to share their words with the world.

To everyone else from past teachers, graduate school friends, river acquaintances, casting instructors, adventure guides and buddies, thank you. Thank you for sharing your knowledge wholeheartedly, welcoming and teaching all of us newbies in the community, and being willing to share your passion and love for the outdoors with others. Your impact goes beyond what you can know, and fosters a passion for this earth and the natural world that is home to us all.

NOTES

NOTES

NOTES

NOTES

Made in the USA
Middletown, DE
27 March 2025